REAL WORLD D...

GRAPHING THE ENVIRONMENT

Andrew Solway

Heinemann LIBRARY

www.heinemann.co.uk/library
Visit our website to find out more information about **Heinemann Library** books.

To order:
☎ Phone 44 (0) 1865 888066
▤ Send a fax to 44 (0) 1865 314091
▢ Visit the Heinemann Bookshop at www.heinemann.co.uk/library to browse our catalogue and order online.

Heinemann Library is an imprint of Pearson Education Limited, a company incorporated in England and Wales having its registered office at Edinburgh Gate, Harlow, Essex, CM20 2JE – Registered company number: 00872828
Heinemann Library is a registered trademark of Pearson Education Limited
Text © Pearson Education Ltd 2009
First published in hardback in 2009
First published in paperback in 2009
The moral rights of the proprietor have been asserted.

Edited by Nancy Dickmann, Rachel Howells, and Sian Smith
Designed by Victoria Bevan and Geoff Ward
Illustrated by Geoff Ward
Picture Research by Mica Brancic and Elaine Willis
Originated by Modern Age
Printed and bound in China by Leo Paper Group

13-digit ISBN 978 0 431 02953 5 (hardback)
13 12 11 10 09
10 9 8 7 6 5 4 3 2 1

13-digit ISBN 978 0 431 02967 2 (paperback)
13 12 11 10 09
10 9 8 7 6 5 4 3 2 1

British Library Cataloguing in Publication Data
Solway, Andrew
  Graphing the environment. - (Real world data)
  363.7'00728

A full catalogue record for this book is available from the British Library.

Acknowledgements
The publishers would like to thank the following for permission to reproduce photographs:
© Alamy pp.**6** (David Ball), **15** (Ern Mainka), **20** (Keith Douglas), **22** (AfriPics.com); © Corbis pp.**4** (NASA), **9** (Jonathan Blair), **11** (NASA), **13** (Gideon Mendel), **14** (Richard Hamilton Smith), **16** (Carol Cohen), **19** (Reuters, China Photos), **24** (epa, Alex Hoffman), **25** (© Wu Dongjun, epa), **26** (Javier Barbancho, Reuters); © Getty Images pp. **10** (Aurora, Peter Essick), **27** (AFP, Daniel Garcia)

Cover photograph of grey glacier, reproduced with permission of ©Getty Images (Taxi).

Every effort has been made to contact copyright holders of any material reproduced in this book. Any omissions will be rectified in subsequent printings if notice is given to the publishers.

The publishers would like to thank Harold Pratt for his assistance in the preparation of this book.

Disclaimer
All the Internet addresses (URLs) given in this book were valid at time of going to press. However, due to the dynamic nature of the Internet, some addresses may have changed, or sites may have changed or ceased to exist since publication. While the author and publishers regret any inconvenience this may cause readers, no responsibility for any such changes can be accepted by either the author or the publishers. It is recommended that adults supervise children on the Internet.

CONTENTS

Some words are printed in bold, **like this**. You can find out what they mean by looking in the glossary, on page 30.

From space, Earth is a blue-green jewel, decorated with white clouds. On this ball of water and rock, billions of people, animals, and plants live together. Most of these living things survive by **adapting** to the **environment** that they live in. However, humans have survived by adapting the environment to suit them. For thousands of years this has worked very well. Human populations have grown and spread.

In the last 150 years or so, the changes we have made to our environment have begun to have bad effects. We have started to destroy the **natural resources** that make life on Earth possible. Air, water, **fertile** land, and the other living things on the planet have all been damaged by human activities. Recently, scientific studies have made it clear that we cannot go on the way we have been.

 The Earth is an island of life in the darkness of space. If we destroy its natural resources, we cannot get more from elsewhere.

Why do we use graphs?

Often, scientific information (**data**) is in the form of numbers. When we look at data of this kind, it can be hard to understand. Graphs and charts present data visually, which helps us to see patterns.

Line graphs are good for showing sets of related information, or for showing how something changes over time. This table and line graph below show the rainfall over the year for Bangkok and New York. We can see that rainfall in Bangkok varies far more over the year than it does in New York.

Month	Rainfall (mm)	
	New York, USA	Bangkok, Thailand
Jan	143	11
Feb	76	26
Mar	169	31
Apr	131	72
May	131	189
Jun	51	152
Jul	113	158
Aug	83	187
Sep	59	320
Oct	86	231
Nov	103	57
Dec	107	9

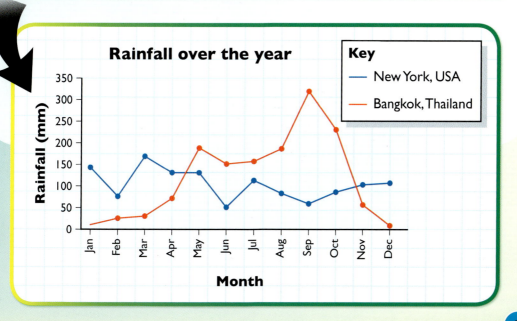

MORE AND MORE PEOPLE

There are over 6 billion (6,000 million) people in the world today. Every day more people are born, and the population of the world continues to rise.

Growing fast

World population is growing much faster today than in the past. It took until 1804 – over 10,000 years of human history – for the world population to reach one billion. However, in the last 200 years or so the population has increased to over six times this figure.

Population is growing faster now because we have become much better at growing food and preventing illness. Fewer people die from disease or starvation, so the population keeps growing. We may recently have passed the peak of population growth. Overall, the population is not growing quite so fast now as it was in the 1960s. However, the population in regions such as South America and Africa are set to continue rising for many years yet.

 This is a crowded swimming pool in Tokyo, Japan. The centre of Tokyo has become increasingly congested. Over 11 million commuters pour into Tokyo to work every day.

Extra resources

Having more and more people on the planet means using more and more of its resources. Each new person needs somewhere to live, food to eat, clothes to wear, and many other things. Finding enough space, **energy**, and materials for all these people becomes more difficult as the population increases.

Graph axes

A graph has two axes, an **x-axis** and a **y-axis**. The horizontal x-axis runs along the bottom of the graph. The vertical y-axis runs up the side. Usually the groups or categories we are looking at are placed along the x-axis, and the values for each group or category are placed on the y-axis.

On this graph, population is on the y-axis because this is the value that is changing year by year. The graph shows that the world population is growing at different rates in different areas. In Asia and Africa it is growing rapidly. However in Europe and North America population is hardly growing, and is predicted to fall by 2050.

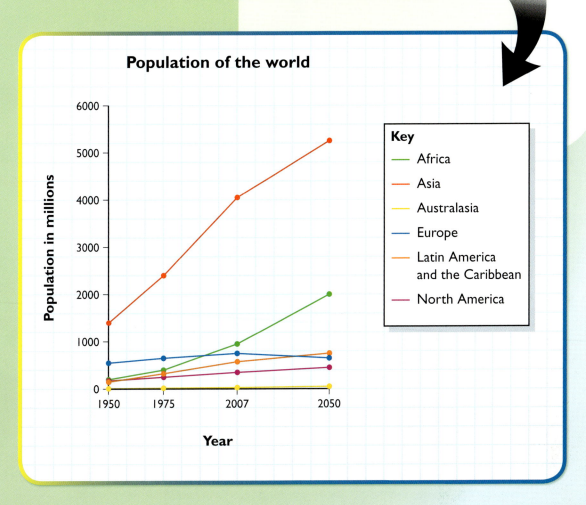

Population of the world

Key
- Africa
- Asia
- Australasia
- Europe
- Latin America and the Caribbean
- North America

In modern society, everyone uses **energy**. We need energy to heat buildings, cook food, to transport people and **goods** around, and for machines and other devices such as computers and lights. We also need energy to make things, and to produce the **raw materials** that we make things from. Getting this energy and using it has a large impact on the **environment**.

Getting energy

Most of our energy comes from **fossil fuels** – oil, gas, and coal. Getting oil, gas, or coal from the ground, or from under the sea, can cause all kinds of environmental problems. Coal-mining, for instance, produces large heaps containing millions of tonnes of slag (mining waste), while leaking pipelines and oil spills at sea can also cause widespread environmental damage.

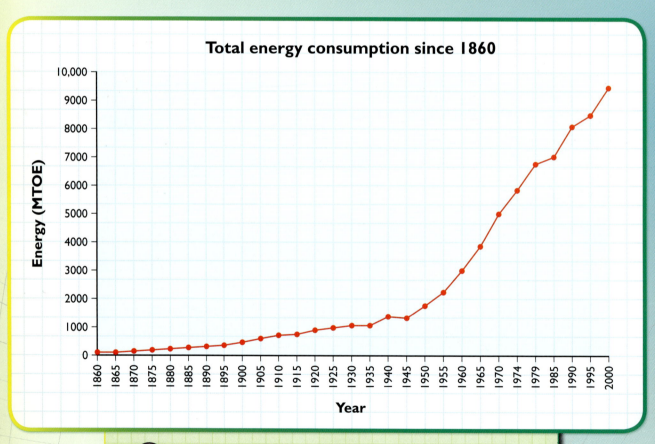

Total energy consumption since 1860

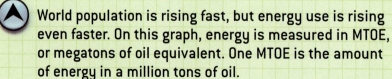

World population is rising fast, but energy use is rising even faster. On this graph, energy is measured in MTOE, or megatons of oil equivalent. One MTOE is the amount of energy in a million tons of oil.

 Bulldozers dig for copper at an opencast copper mine in Cyprus. Opencast mining leaves scars on the landscape, and leaves **pollution** in the ground.

The impact of energy

For about 200 years, fossil fuels have provided us with plenty of cheap energy. This has made it possible for us to do things that need a lot of energy. For example, we have mined for raw materials such as metals on a large scale. Mining damages the environment in several ways.

The mines and associated roads and buildings can destroy large areas of land. The land around the mine can become **contaminated** or poisoned with harmful chemicals. Mining waste can also get into nearby water and contaminate it. If the water is a river, the contamination may be carried far downstream.

POLLUTING THE AIR

The biggest problem with the way we produce **energy** today is that burning **fossil fuels** causes air **pollution**. Air is a mixture of nitrogen, oxygen, and small amounts of other gases. Burning fossil fuels releases other gases into the **atmosphere**, and this affects the **environment**.

Polluting gases

The main gas produced when fossil fuels burn is carbon dioxide. Small amounts of this gas are found naturally in the air, but large amounts act as a pollutant. The effects of this are described on pages 12–13. Other polluting gases produced include ones containing sulphur and nitrogen. These gases cause **smog** in cities, and they can give people lung problems if there is too much in the air.

Acid rain

Sulphur and nitrogen oxides are soluble (they **dissolve** in water). When it rains, some of these oxides dissolve in the raindrops. The result is that the rain is slightly **acid**.

Acid rain has many effects, particularly on rivers and lakes. It can harm or kill many of the plants and animals that live in the water. In extreme cases, all the fish in a lake may be killed. Acid rain has other effects, too. In forests, trees are damaged or even die. In cities and towns acid rain causes damage to buildings, bridges, and vehicles.

 The enormous iron and steelworks in Magnitogorsk, Russia, has made the city one of the most polluted in the world.

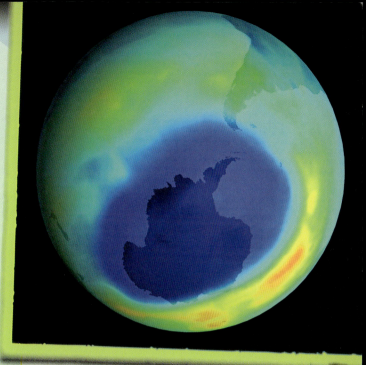

Holes in the ozone layer

Ozone is a kind of oxygen. It is found mostly high in the atmosphere, where it protects us from harmful rays from the sun. Certain types of gases used in, for example, spray cans, break down ozone in the atmosphere. In recent years, this thinned the ozone layer, allowing more harmful radiation to reach the surface.

 In recent years, the ozone layer over the Antarctic has become so thin that each spring a "hole" forms where there is no ozone at all. In 2000 the hole (in blue) was the largest yet seen.

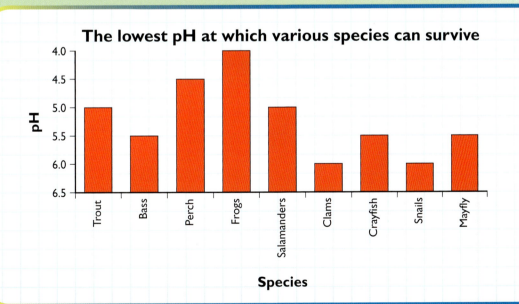

The lowest pH at which various species can survive

pH / Species
(bar chart)
Trout, Bass, Perch, Frogs, Salamanders, Clams, Crayfish, Snails, Mayfly

 Some water animals can survive in more acid conditions than others. This bar chart shows the lowest **pH** at which several **species** can survive. Water is normally around pH 7. A lower pH indicates more acid water.

When sunlight reaches the Earth's surface, some is **absorbed** (taken in) and some is reflected as heat **energy**. Part of the reflected energy escapes into space, but some is trapped by gases in the **atmosphere**. The trapped heat helps keep the Earth warm.

Carbon dioxide is one of the gases that trap the sun's heat. Because we are producing more carbon dioxide by burning **fossil fuels**, more of the sun's warmth is being trapped. The result is that the Earth's **climate** is getting warmer.

Climate change

A global increase in temperature will have many unwelcome effects. The ice around the North and South Poles has already started melting. As more ice melts, sea levels will rise. This will cause more flooding, and some places may disappear underwater.

The warmer climate is also changing the world's weather patterns. In some areas, there will be more rainfall. In other areas, low rainfall will turn farmland to desert. Climate change also makes weather such as hurricanes and rainstorms more likely.

Some of the sunlight that reaches the Earth is absorbed by the ground, then re-emitted as heat. The atmosphere stops some of this heat from escaping into space. This is known as the greenhouse effect.

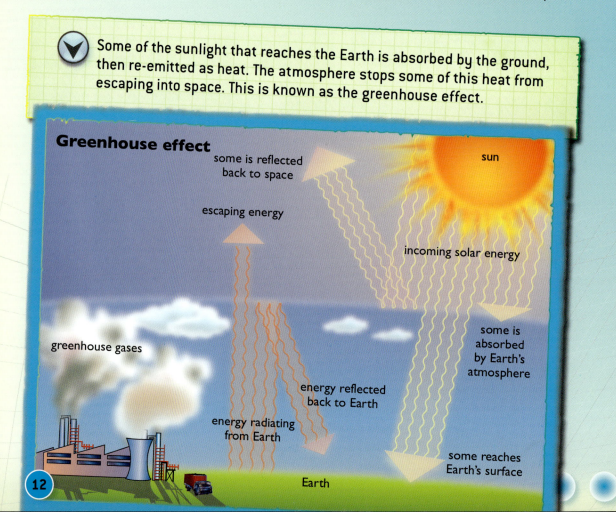

Greenhouse effect

some is reflected back to space

sun

escaping energy

incoming solar energy

greenhouse gases

some is absorbed by Earth's atmosphere

energy reflected back to Earth

energy radiating from Earth

some reaches Earth's surface

Earth

Change in the Arctic

The Arctic is actually a huge frozen ocean. Each spring part of this enormous ice sheet melts, then freezes again in winter. In recent years, the ice has melted earlier each spring and spread less far in the winter. As a result, the **habitat** of polar bears, seals, Arctic foxes, and other wildlife has been greatly reduced. These animals will either have to **adapt** to the changing **climate** or die out.

 This line graph shows how average temperatures have gradually increased since 1880. Although the values go up and down nearly all years since about 1935 have been above the long-term average (0 on the **y-axis**).

 This shows flooding in Upton-on-Severn, UK, in 2007. Such flooding will become more common as the Earth gets warmer.

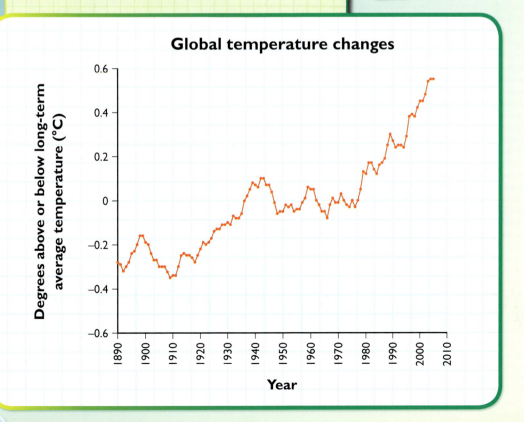

Global temperature changes

DAMAGING THE LAND

Supporting six billion people has put a great strain on the land. Like the **atmosphere**, the land has been damaged by **pollution** and human activities.

Growing crops

With so many mouths to feed, farming is a very important use of the land. About 15 million square kilometres (6 million square miles) of land is used to grow crops. Large areas of forest and other **habitats** have been destroyed to create farmland.

Modern farming methods have been successful, but they are causing long-term damage to land. For example, when crops are harvested and fields are left bare, soil is eroded (washed or blown away).

Nearly one-third of the world's croplands have been lost through erosion in the past 40 years. In hot countries, misuse of land can cause **desertification**, where the soil turns to dust and farmland turns into desert.

 Although some people do go hungry today, it is because food is not distributed evenly. With modern farming methods it is possible to produce enough food for everyone.

 Several years of drought, and over-grazing the land, has turned this area of the Flinders Ranges in South Australia into desert.

Bar chart

A bar chart is a good way of comparing groups, for example different continents. In a stacked bar chart, different values are stacked one on top of another. This graph shows the percentage of land on each continent with soil damage. The overall height shows the total amount of land damaged. The different parts of the stack indicate whether the damage is light, medium, or severe.

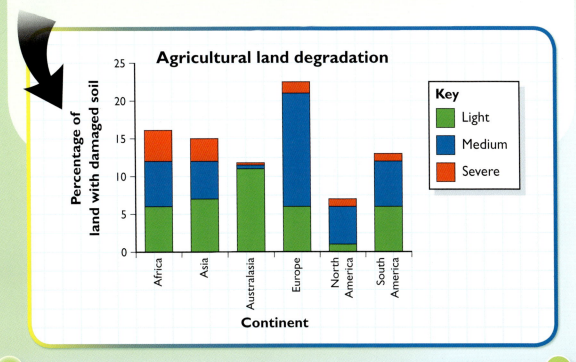

People need water even more than they need food. Without water, we would die in just a few days. Each person needs about 4 litres of water a day. However, we use water for much more than just drinking.

Other uses

In **developed countries** people use water in many ways. The biggest use is for **irrigation** (watering crops). Seventy percent of all the water supply goes to irrigate farmland. Water is also used in industry and in power stations. At home, we use water to shower or bathe, wash clothes, flush the toilet, and water the garden. All these uses can add up to between 2,000 and 5,000 litres each day per person.

 One of the most effective ways to reduce world water use would be the widespread use of drip irrigation. This is an irrigation method that minimizes the use of water by allowing it to drip slowly to the plant roots.

Effects on the environment

We use so much water that the amount of fresh water available is being reduced. Many large rivers are dammed to make **reservoirs**. Much of the water in the reservoirs is used for irrigation and for drinking water. The result is that water flow is reduced below the dam. So much water is taken from rivers such as the Colorado in the United States and the Yellow River in China, that they have hardly any water left in them when they reach the sea. The amount of water underground (ground water) is also falling.

Pie charts

Pie charts are usually the best way to show how something is divided up. Each piece of the circle, or "pie", is a percentage of the whole. This pie chart shows the different ways we use the water that comes into our homes.

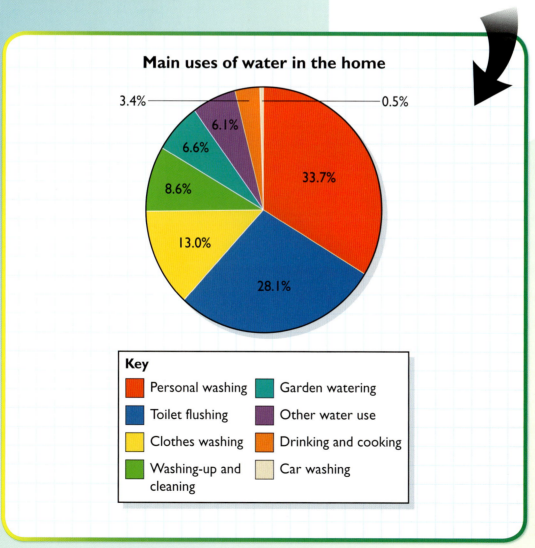

Main uses of water in the home

3.4% — 6.1% 6.6% 8.6% 13.0% 28.1% 33.7% 0.5%

Key

- ■ Personal washing
- ■ Toilet flushing
- ■ Clothes washing
- ■ Washing-up and cleaning
- ■ Garden watering
- ■ Other water use
- ■ Drinking and cooking
- ■ Car washing

Wherever you look on the Earth, there are living things. Even in the Antarctic or in the depths of dark caves, there are some kinds of living things. About 1.5 million different types of living things have been described, and scientists estimate that there at least 10 million in total. This incredible variety of life is known as **biodiversity**.

Survival of life

Without biodiversity, life on Earth would not have survived for so long. Over the last 500 million years, global disasters have caused several **mass extinctions**, in which huge numbers of animal and plant **species** died out. The worst extinction was about 251 million years ago. It killed off 95 percent of all sea life and 70 percent of life on land. However, because of biodiversity, some species did survive to repopulate the Earth.

 Over the last 500 million years there have been six periods when extinction rates were high.

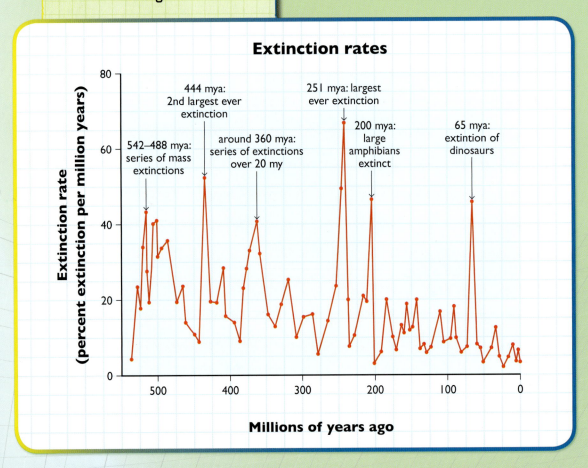

Extinction rates

Extinction rate (percent extinction per million years)

542–488 mya: series of mass extinctions

444 mya: 2nd largest ever extinction

around 360 mya: series of extinctions over 20 my

251 mya: largest ever extinction

200 mya: large amphibians extinct

65 mya: extinction of dinosaurs

Millions of years ago

 The Chinese alligator is one of many endangered species. A species is endangered if its population is falling, and experts think that the species could die out altogether.

New extinctions

We are now in the middle of another mass extinction like those in the past. Species are becoming extinct 50 to 100 times faster than normal, and this rate is likely to increase in the future. The disaster causing this mass extinction is human activity.

Habitat loss

Pollution and over-hunting or fishing of animals for food are among the activities that have reduced biodiversity. However, the main cause is changes to the landscape, which have destroyed the **habitats** of many species. The effects of human activities on different habitats are described on the following pages.

Forests are the Earth's most important land **habitats**. A huge number of animal and plant **species** live in forests, especially tropical **rainforests**. The trees and other plants also produce vast quantities of oxygen, which is essential for renewing the **atmosphere**.

Fewer forests

Eight thousand years ago, almost half the world was covered with forest. Today, forest covers only a quarter of the land. Forest areas have been cleared for farmland, for buildings or roads, to supply trees for building or for paper-making. In tropical areas, many sections of original forest areas have been replaced by **plantations**. These contain only one or a few types of tree, and they support less **biodiversity**. This means that far fewer species of animals and plants live there than in the original forest.

 These hills in Madagascar were once completely covered by rainforest. Today, rainforest in Madagascar covers less than half the area it did in 1950.

Protecting forests

One way of slowing the loss of forests is to protect areas that are high in biodiversity. Currently about 12 percent of all forests are protected. However, most of these are in North America and Europe. To save forest diversity, we need to protect more of the rich rainforest areas in Asia, Africa, and South America.

Ecotourism

Another approach that could save rainforest areas is ecotourism. This is a form of tourism that takes people to undisturbed natural areas to see the wildlife. When ecotourism is successful, the undisturbed rainforest becomes more valuable than the land would be if it was used for growing crops or as a plantation.

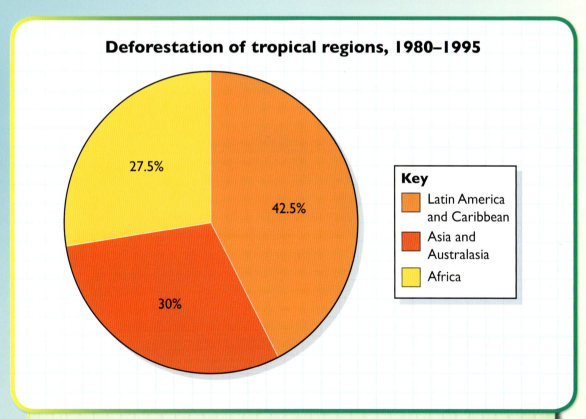

Deforestation of tropical regions, 1980–1995

- 27.5%
- 42.5%
- 30%

Key
- Latin America and Caribbean
- Asia and Australasia
- Africa

 Between 1980 and 1995, 1.8 million square kilometres of tropical forest were lost. This is more than the areas of Spain, France, and Germany combined. This pie chart shows how much of this loss happened in each continent.

The oceans cover over two-thirds of the Earth's surface and probably contain more **biodiversity** than the land. The "plants" of the ocean are tiny creatures called plankton. Like plants, some of the plankton produce oxygen. They also **absorb** (soak up) about a third of the carbon dioxide produced from burning **fossil fuels**. The huge variety of ocean life, from shrimps to whales, is supported by the plankton.

Mangrove swamps like this one in South Africa are rich in biodiversity. They also protect coasts from flooding.

Pollution and overfishing

Most of the **pollution** we produce ends up in the oceans. All kinds of chemicals and wastes that are released into rivers eventually find their way to the sea and pollute coastal waters. Pollution from **acid** rain, oil spills, and toxic (poisonous) chemicals also pollute the oceans.

Another problem caused by human activities is over-fishing. Large fishing boats lay nets and lines that stretch over many kilometres. As well as catching huge numbers of fish, this type of fishing traps other marine life. Dolphins and many other sea creatures are killed this way.

Mangroves and corals

Mangrove swamps and **coral reefs** are two of richest **habitats** on Earth. However, both are disappearing at an alarming rate. Mangrove swamps have been badly affected by over-farming. Shrimp farms have been set up in many mangrove areas, and this involves clearing the mangroves.

The biggest threat to coral reefs is **climate** change. Coral reefs are found in warm shallow seas, but the corals cannot survive if they get too warm. Many areas of coral reef have become bleached (gone white) and died because the temperature of the water has risen too high.

Line of best fit

This graph shows the changes in average sea levels between 1993 and 2006. Like all line graphs it was created by plotting **data** points and connecting these with a line. The graph is complicated, and the sea levels go up and down. However, if we draw a line of best fit (shown in blue) through the graph, we can see that sea levels are steadily rising. Part of this rise is due to warming of the oceans.

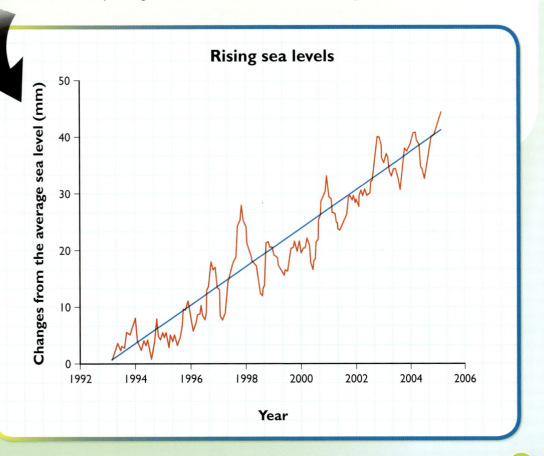

Rising sea levels

Changes from the average sea level (mm)

Year

In a relatively small area, rivers, lakes, and **wetlands** support a huge number of different plants and animals. The fish and other **species** that live there are more under threat than species on land or in the oceans.

Packed with species

Less than 3 percent of the world's water is freshwater. Yet this tiny fraction contains 40 percent of the world's fish species. Wetlands are important **habitats** for many insects and for migrating birds. They also remove toxic (harmful) substances from water, and act as "sponges" that help to prevent flooding.

Freshwater threats

Rivers, lakes, and wetlands are being damaged in several ways. Water is being polluted by chemicals and wastes. Most of this comes from water draining from fields or from cities, polluted with substances such as oil and chemicals used in farming.

Over-fishing is also causing **biodiversity** loss. And changes to rivers, such as dam-building, destroy habitats for many river species. Dams have had a huge effect on wildlife. For example many fish species in the lower Colorado River in the United States, have either died out or are highly endangered. The river has so many dams that there is hardly any water left for the fish to live in.

The Baiji, or Yangtze river dolphin, is found only in China's Yangtze river. It is now so rare that there has only been one definite sighting since 2004.

Unwanted intruders

In some areas animal and plant species that do not belong have been introduced and have caused **environmental** problems. In the African lakes Victoria and Malawi, for example, the Nile perch was introduced as a food fish. The perch has eaten many of the cichlid fish that are **native** to the lakes. Nearly half the cichlids are now **extinct** or extremely rare.

 The water hyacinth is native to South America, but humans have spread it to many other areas. If unchecked it blocks waterways and kills fish and other water species.

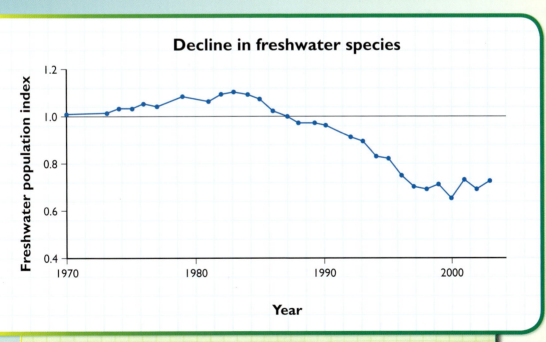

Decline in freshwater species

Freshwater population index vs *Year*

 The Freshwater Index measures how populations of freshwater animals have changed worldwide since 1970 (1970 has a value of 1.0). The index shows an overall drop in freshwater populations of around 30 per cent.

TREADING LIGHTLY ON THE EARTH

In the past, humans trod lightly on the Earth – they lived without having a large effect on the **environment** around them. We need to find ways to do this today.

Finding solutions

Scientists and other people have been working to try and limit or reverse environmental damage. New forms of **energy**, such as solar (sun) power and wind energy do not produce carbon dioxide, as **fossil fuels** do, and they will not run out. New buildings are being designed that need very little energy for heating or lighting. Waste is being reduced by recycling, or making it into useful products. Areas of **rainforest** and other places with high **biodiversity** are being protected. Water-saving **processes** such as drip **irrigation** can reduce water use.

Such solutions are not yet used widely enough to improve the environment. But things are beginning to change. Politicians and governments are starting to get involved in protecting the environment. Hopefully this will continue in the future.

 These mirrors are part of Europe's first solar thermal power station, near Seville, Spain.

US President George Bush Senior speaks at the Earth Summit in Brazil, 1992. President Bush signed the Kyoto Protocol in 1992, but when his son became US President in 2001 he withdrew from the agreement.

Kyoto and beyond

In 1992, the Earth Summit was held in Rio de Janeiro. Important government officials from 172 countries met to try and agree ways to combat **climate** change. One of the agreements that came out of the Summit was the Kyoto Protocol. In the Protocol 36 **developed countries** agreed to reduce their greenhouse gas emissions by 2012. Not all countries signed up to the Kyoto Protocol, and the reductions agreed were not large enough. However, it was a first step towards combating climate change.

Since 1992 negotiations to develop an improved climate change agreement have been held each year, with mixed results. At the 2007 Climate Change Conference in Bali all governments, including the United States, agreed to finalise a blueprint by 2009 for what countries will do to fight climate change after 2012, when the Kyoto Protocol runs out.

Data is information about something. We often get important data as a mass of numbers, and it can be difficult to make sense of them. Graphs and charts are ways of displaying information visually. This helps us to see relationships and patterns in the data. Different types of graphs or charts are good for displaying different types of information.

Pie charts

A pie chart is used to show the different parts of a whole picture. A pie chart is the best way to show how something is divided up. These charts show information as different sized portions of a circle. They can help you compare proportions. You can easily see which section is the largest slice of the "pie".

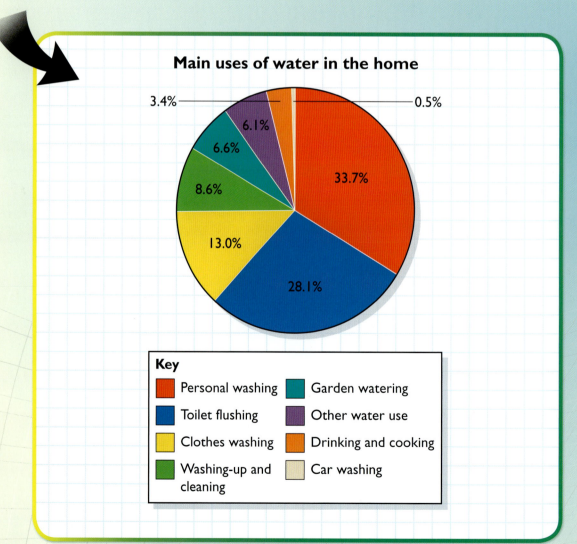

Main uses of water in the home

- 3.4%
- 0.5%
- 6.1%
- 6.6%
- 33.7%
- 8.6%
- 13.0%
- 28.1%

Key

■ Personal washing	■ Garden watering
■ Toilet flushing	■ Other water use
■ Clothes washing	■ Drinking and cooking
■ Washing-up and cleaning	■ Car washing

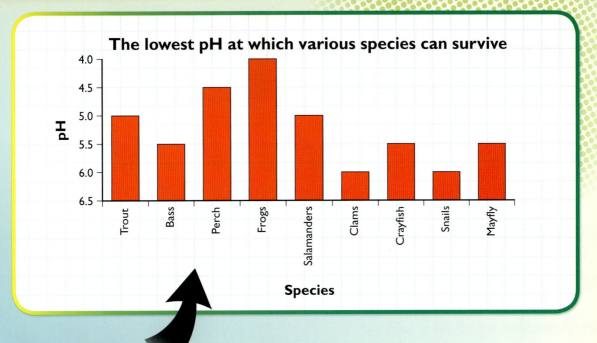

The lowest pH at which various species can survive

Bar charts

Bar charts are a good way to compare amounts of different things. Bar charts have a vertical **y-axis** showing the **frequency**, and a horizontal **x-axis** showing the different types of information. They can show one or more different types of bars.

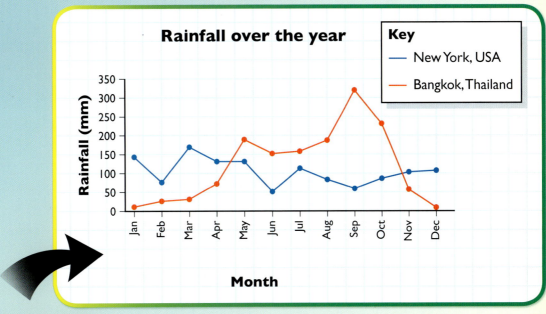

Rainfall over the year

Line graphs

Line graphs use lines to join up points on a graph. They can be used to show how something changes over time. If you put several lines on one line graph, you can compare the overall pattern of several sets of data. Time, such as months, is usually shown on the x-axis.

GLOSSARY

absorb take in or soak up

acid substance that has a pH of less than 7. Weak acids taste sour, strong acids can dissolve metal.

adapt change to fit in

atmosphere layer of air that surrounds the Earth

biodiversity variety of living things

climate general weather of an area over a long period of time

contaminate to make dirty or impure

coral reef underwater structure of rock-like material, made by living things called corals

data information, often in the form of numbers

desertification process in which previously fertile land becomes desert

developed country country where most people live in towns and have a fairly good standard of living

dissolve mix a substance completely with water so that it is no longer visible

energy ability to do work, for example powering a car or a light

environment our surroundings and external conditions

extinct when a species of living things dies out completely

fertile (land) land that is good for growing crops

fossil fuel oil, gas, or coal

frequency number of things in a group of data

goods any products that are bought and sold, or transported from place to place

habitat place where an animal or plant lives

irrigation artificial method for watering farm crops

mangrove type of tree that can grow in salty, waterlogged ground

mass extinction time when large numbers of species of living things die out altogether

native belonging to a particular place

natural resources raw materials supplied by the Earth

pH measure of how acid or alkaline a liquid is

plantation large farm, usually in a tropical area, where crops such as coffee, tea, cotton, rubber, or palm oil are grown

pollution when substances get into the environment and damage it

process way of doing something

rainforest type of forest in warm, tropical regions where there is a large amount of rainfall all year round

raw material natural substance from the ground, from water, or from the air which is used to make things

reservoir artificial lake made by damming a river or stream

smog type of dirty fog caused by air pollution

species group of similar living things that can breed together

wetland a marsh, swamp, or other area where the ground is waterlogged for most or all of the year

x-axis horizontal line on a graph

y-axis vertical line on a graph

FURTHER INFORMATION

Books

Our Fragile World: The Beauty Of A Planet Under Pressure, Troth Wells and Caspar Henderson (Thames and Hudson, 2005)

Planet Under Pressure: Animals Under Threat, Louise Spilsbury (Raintree, 2006)

Planet Under Pressure: Food, Paul Mason (Raintree, 2006)

Planet Under Pressure: Pollution, Clive Gifford (Raintree, 2006)

Rainforest, Thomas Marent (Dorling Kindersley, 2006)

Sustainable Futures: Energy, John Stringer (Evans Brothers, 2005)

Websites

Look at satellite photos of the Earth from space and read the explanations of them to find out about the Earth and the impact humans are having on it.
www.earthfromspace.si.edu/online_exhibition.asp

The Living Planet Report 2006, from the World Wildlife Fund provides information on how other living things on the planet are affected by human actions.
www.panda.org/news_facts/publications/living_planet_report/index.cfm

Visit Visible Earth for images of the Earth from the National Aeronautics and Space Administration (NASA).
visibleearth.nasa.gov

INDEX